THE COMPANY

Kate Duchene   Anastasia Hille
Kristin Hutchinson   Sean Jackson
Stephen Kennedy   Liz Kettle
Paul Ready   Jonah Russell

Michael Gould was part of the original ensemble who devised the production.

DIRECTOR Katie Mitchell

LIGHTING DESIGNER Paule Constable

MUSIC Paul Clark

SOUND DESIGNER Gareth Fry

DESIGNER Vicki Mortimer

VIDEO DESIGNER/CINEMATOGRAPHER Leo Warner

MUSIC DIRECTOR & ARRANGER Simon Allen

TAP-DANCE COACH Donna Berlin/Scott Cripps

Waves opened at the National Theate's Cottesloe Theatre on 18 November 2006; the production was revived in the Cottesloe on 20 August 2008, before touring nationally and internationally.

WAVES

A record of the multimedia work devised by Katie Mitchell and the company
from the text of Virginia Woolf's novel *The Waves*

OBERON BOOKS

Waves published in 2008 by Oberon Books Ltd

521 Caledonian Road, London N7 9RH

Tel: 020 7607 3637 / Fax: 020 7607 3629

e-mail: info@oberonbooks.com

www.oberonbooks.com

Designed and typeset by Libanus Press, Marlborough

Printed in Great Britain by Hampton Printing (Bristol) Ltd

National Theatre, South Bank, London SE1 9PX

www.nationaltheatre.org.uk

Foreword

The images in this book are those that were output live to the projection screen during the performance. They were created on the stage beneath the projection screen by the ensemble using video cameras, lights, props and costumes. The book does not contain any photographs of the actors' work at stage level. Neither does the book contain descriptions of the audio passages in the performance. For example, the actors did the sound effects of people running for trains, doors opening or closing, the movement of clothing, the noise of eating and so on. These sounds were laid over sections of the text or synchronised with specific movements in the video pictures. The text is made up almost entirely of extracts from Virginia Woolf's novel, *The Waves*, written in 1931. There are also a few paragraphs from her book *Moments of Being* and these are printed in blue type.

Katie Mitchell
Director

ONE

As they neared the shore each bar rose, heaped itself, broke and swept a thin veil of white water across the sand. The wave paused, and then drew out again, sighing like a sleeper whose breath comes and goes unconsciously. Gradually the dark bar on the horizon became clear. The surface of the sea slowly became transparent and lay rippling and sparkling until the dark stripes were almost rubbed out.

The light struck upon the trees in the garden, making one leaf transparent and then another. The sun sharpened the walls of the house, and rested like the tip of a fan upon a white blind and made a blue finger-print of shadow under the leaf by the bedroom window. The blind stirred slightly, but all within was dim and unsubstantial. The birds sang their blank melody outside.

◖ If I were a painter I should paint these first impressions of childhood in pale yellow, silver, and green. I should make a picture of curved petals; of shells; of things that were semi-transparent. Everything would be large and dim; and what was seen would at the same time be heard; sounds would come through this petal or leaf – sounds indistinguishable from sights. Sound and sight seem to make equal parts of these first impressions. ◖

'Look at the house,' said Jinny, 'with all its windows white with blinds.'

'The dining-room window is dark blue now,' said Bernard, 'and the air ripples above the chimneys.'

'A swallow is perched on the lightning-conductor,' said Susan. 'And Biddy has smacked down the bucket on the kitchen flags.'

'Suddenly a bee booms in my ear,' said Neville. 'It is here; it is past.'

'The leaves are gathered round the window like pointed ears,' said Susan.

'A shadow falls on the path,' said Louis, 'like an elbow bent'.

'Islands of light are swimming on the grass,' said Rhoda. 'They have fallen through the trees.'

'The birds' eyes are bright in the tunnels between the leaves,' said Neville.

'The stalks are covered with harsh, short hairs,' said Jinny, 'and drops of water have stuck to them.'

'A caterpillar is curled in a green ring,' said Susan, 'notched with blunt feet.'

'Stones are cold to my feet,' said Neville. 'I feel each one, round or pointed, separately.'

'The grey-shelled snail draws across the path and flattens the blades behind him,' said Rhoda.

'And burning lights from the window-panes flash in and out on the grasses,' said Louis.

'The back of my hand burns,' said Jinny, 'but the palm is clammy and damp with dew.'

'Look at the spider's web on the corner of the balcony,' said Bernard. 'It has beads of water on it, drops of white light.'

'I burn, I shiver,' said Jinny, 'out of this sun, into this shadow.'

'I hear something stamping,' said Louis. 'A great beast's foot is chained. It stamps, and stamps, and stamps.'

'Now they have all gone,' said Louis. 'I am alone. I am on the other side of the hedge. There are only little eye-holes among the leaves. I am the stalk. My roots go down to the depths of the world, through earth dry with brick, and damp earth, through veins of lead and silver. I am all fibre. I am a boy in grey flannels with a belt fastened by a brass snake up here. Down there my eyes are the lidless eyes of a stone figure in a desert by the Nile. I see women passing with red pitchers to the river; I see camels swaying and men in turbans.'

'Oh Lord, let them pass. Lord, let them lay their butterflies on a pocket-handkerchief on the gravel. Let them count out their tortoise-shells, their red admirals and cabbage whites. But let me be unseen. Now an eye-beam is slid through the chink. Its beam strikes me. She has found me. All is shattered.'

'I saw leaves moving in a hole in the hedge', said Jinny. 'That is a bird on its nest. There was no bird on its nest. What moved the leaves? The leaves go on moving. I dashed in here. The leaves go on moving. "Is he dead?" I thought.'

'Through the chink in the hedge,' said Susan, 'I saw her kiss him. I raised my head from my flower-pot and looked through a chink in the hedge. I saw her kiss him. I saw them, Jinny and Louis, kissing.'

'Now I will wrap my agony inside my pocket-handkerchief. It shall be screwed tight into a ball. I will go to the beech wood alone. I will take my anguish and lay it upon the roots under the beech trees. I will examine it and take it between my fingers. They will not find me. I shall eat nuts and peer for eggs through the brambles and my hair will be matted and I shall sleep under hedges and drink water from ditches and die there.'

'Susan has passed us,' said Bernard. 'She has passed the tool-house door with her handkerchief screwed into a ball. She was not crying, but her eyes, which are so beautiful, were narrow as cats' eyes before they spring. I shall follow her, Neville, to comfort her when she bursts out in a rage and thinks, "I am alone".'

'I saw her kiss him,' said Susan. 'I looked between the leaves and saw her. She danced in flecked with diamonds light as dust. And I am squat, Bernard, I am short. I have eyes that look close to the ground and see insects in the grass. The yellow warmth in my side turned to stone when I saw Jinny kiss Louis.'

'Now,' said Bernard, 'let us explore. There is the white house lying among the trees. It lies down there ever so far beneath us. We shall sink like swimmers just touching the ground with the tips of their toes. We shall sink through the green air of the leaves, Susan. We sink as we run. The waves close over us, the beech leaves meet above our heads.

'Now we are in the ringed wood with the wall round it. The ferns smell very strong, and there are red funguses growing beneath them. Listen! That is the flop of a giant toad in the undergrowth; that is the patter of some primeval fir-cone falling to rot among the ferns.'

'Look over the wall. There is the stable clock with its gilt hands shining. There is the stable-boy clattering in the yard in rubber boots. That is Elvedon. That is the close-clipped hedge of the ladies' garden. There they walk at noon, with scissors, clipping roses. That is Elvedon. The lady sits between the two long windows, writing. The gardeners sweep the lawn with giant brooms. We are the first to come here. We are the discoverers of an unknown land. Do not stir; if the gardeners saw us they would shoot us. We should be nailed like stoats to the stable door. Look! Do not move. Grasp the ferns tight on the top of the wall.'

'I see the lady writing. I see the gardeners sweeping,' said Susan. 'If we died here, nobody would bury us.'

'Run!' said Bernard. 'Run! The gardener with the black beard has seen us! We shall be shot! We shall be shot like jays and pinned to the wall! There is a secret path. Bend as low as you can. Follow without looking back. They will think we are foxes. Run!'

'Now we are safe. Now we can stand upright again. Now we can stretch our arms in this high canopy, in this vast wood. I hear nothing. That is only the murmur of the waves in the air. That is a wood-pigeon breaking cover in the tops of the beech trees. The pigeon beats the air; the pigeon beats the air with wooden wings.'

'Where is Bernard?' said Neville. 'He has my knife. He is like a dangling wire, a broken bell-pull, always twangling. I hate dangling things; I hate dampish things. I hate wandering and mixing things together. Here is Rhoda on the path, rocking her petals to and fro in her basin.'

'I have a short time alone, while Miss Hudson spreads our copy-books on the schoolroom table,' said Rhoda. 'I have a short space of freedom. I have picked all the fallen petals and made them swim. I have put raindrops in some. And I will now rock my basin from side to side so that my ships may ride the waves.'

'All my ships are white. They ride the waves. Some founder. Some dash themselves against the cliffs. One sails alone. That is my ship. It sails into icy caverns where the sea-bear barks.'

'Now the bell rings and we shall be late', said Louis. 'Now we must drop our toys. Now we must go in together. The copy-books are laid out side by side on the green baize table. Now they suck their pens. Now they twist their copy-books, and, looking sideways at Miss Hudson, count the purple buttons on her bodice.'

'Now the terror is beginning,' said Rhoda. 'Now Miss Hudson is taking her lump of chalk.'

'They look with understanding. Louis writes; Susan writes; Neville writes; Jinny writes; even Bernard has now begun to write. But I cannot write. I see only figures. The others are handing in their answers, one by one. Now it is my turn. But I have no answer.'

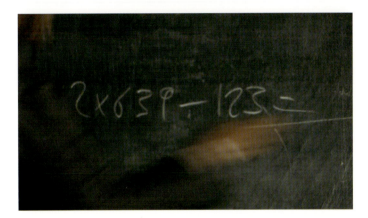

'The others are allowed to go. They slam the door. Miss Hudson goes. I am left alone to find an answer. The figures mean nothing now. Meaning has gone.'

'Look, the loop of the figure is beginning to fill with time; it holds the world in it. I begin to draw a figure and the world is looped in it, and I myself am outside the loop; which I now join – so – and seal up, and make entire. The world is entire, and I am outside of it, crying, Oh save me, from being blown for ever outside the loop of time!'

'Her shoulder-blades meet across her back like the wings of a small butterfly,' said Louis. 'She has no body as the others have. And I, who speak with an Australian accent, whose father is a banker in Brisbane, do not fear her as I fear the others.'

'Things are huge and very small,' said Bernard. 'The stalks of flowers are thick as oak trees. Leaves are high as the domes of vast cathedrals. I am a giant, lying here, who can make forests quiver. The others pass down the carriage-drive. The skirts of Miss Hudson and Miss Curry sweep by like candle extinguishers. Those are Susan's white socks. Those are Louis's neat sandshoes firmly printing the gravel.'

'Miss Curry has blown her whistle on the terrace. I must stand upright.'

'We must walk in order, not shuffling our feet,' said Susan, 'with Louis going first to lead us, because Louis is alert and not a woolgatherer.'

'It is dull,' said Jinny, 'walking along the high road with no windows to look at, with no bleared eyes of blue glass let into the pavement.'

'Since I am supposed,' said Neville, 'to be too delicate to go with them on the walk, since I get so easily tired and then am sick, I will use this hour of solitude, this reprieve from conversation, to coast round the purlieus of the house and recover, if I can, by standing on the same stair half-way up the landing, what I felt when I heard about the dead man through the swing-door last night when cook was shoving in and out the dampers. He was found with his throat cut.'

'The apple-tree leaves became fixed in the sky; the moon glared; I was unable to lift my foot up the stair.'

'He was found in the gutter. His blood gurgled down the gutter. I shall call this "death among the apple trees" for ever. I was unable to pass by. There was an obstacle. And the others passed on. But we are doomed, all of us, by the apple trees, by the immitigable trees which we cannot pass.'

◖ *I hazard the explanation that a shock is at once in my case followed by the desire to explain it. I feel that I have had a blow: but it is not, as I thought as a child, simply a blow from an enemy hidden behind the cotton wool of daily life; it is or will become a revelation of some order; it is a token of some real thing behind appearances; and I make it real by putting it in to words. It is only by putting it in to words that I make it whole; this wholeness means that it has lost its power to hurt me; it gives me, perhaps because by doing so I take away the pain, a great delight to put the severed parts together.* ◖

'I saw Florrie in the kitchen garden,' said Susan, 'as we came back from our walk, with the washing blown out round her, the pyjamas, the drawers.'

'And Ernest kissed her. He was in his green baize apron and his mouth was sucked like a purse in wrinkles and he seized her with the pyjamas blown out hard between them.'

❨ *When I was six or seven perhaps, I got into the habit of looking at my face in the glass. But I only did this if I was sure that I was alone. I was ashamed of it. A strong feeling of guilt seemed naturally attached to it. But why this was so? At any rate the looking glass shame has lasted all my life.* ❩

'Rhoda dreams,' said Susan, 'sucking a crust soaked in milk; Louis regards the wall opposite with snail-green eyes; Bernard moulds his bread into pellets and calls them "people". Neville with his clean and decisive ways has finished. He has rolled his napkin and slipped it through the silver ring. Jinny spins her fingers on the table-cloth, as if they were dancing in the sunshine, pirouetting.'

'It is difficult not to weep,' said Louis, 'as we sing, as we pray that God may keep us safe while we sleep, calling ourselves little children. When we are sad and trembling with apprehension it is sweet to sing together, leaning slightly, I towards Susan, Susan towards Bernard, clasping hands, afraid of much, I of my accent, Rhoda of figures; yet resolute to conquer.'

'We troop upstairs like ponies,' said Bernard, 'stamping, clattering one behind another to take our turns in the bathroom. We buffet, we tussle, we spring up and down on the hard, white beds. My turn has come.'

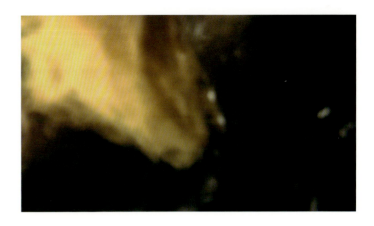

'Mrs Constable, girt in a bath-towel, takes her lemon-coloured sponge and soaks it in water,' said Bernard, 'it turns chocolate-brown; it drips; and, holding it high above me, shivering beneath her, she squeezes it. Water pours down the runnel of my spine. Bright arrows of sensation shoot on either side. Water descends and sheets me like an eel. Down showers the day – the woods; and Elvedon; Susan and the pigeon. Now hot towels envelop me, and their roughness, as I rub my back, makes my blood purr. I tie my pyjamas loosely round me, and lie under this thin sheet afloat in the shallow light which is like a film of water drawn over my eyes by a wave. I hear through it down below Biddy and Mrs Constable clearing the table. I hear through it far off, far away, faint and far, the chorus beginning.'

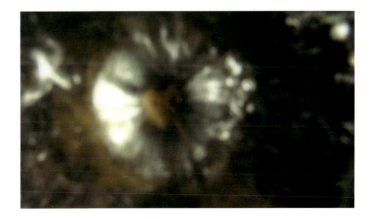

'As I fold up my frock,' said Rhoda, 'so I put off my hopeless desire to be Susan, to be Jinny.'

'But I will assure myself, touching the rail, of something hard. Now I cannot sink; cannot altogether fall through the thin sheet now.'

'Now I spread my body on this frail mattress and hang suspended. I am above the earth now. I am no longer upright, to be knocked against and damaged. Out of me now my mind can pour. I sail on alone under the white cliffs. Oh, but I sink, I fall! That is the corner of the cupboard; that is the nursery looking-glass. I rise over the tree-tops.'

'These waters heap themselves on me; they sweep me between their great shoulders; I am turned; I am tumbled; I am stretched, among these long lights, these long waves, these endless paths, with people pursuing, pursuing.'

'I sink down on the black plumes of sleep; its thick wings are pressed to my eyes.'

TWO

The sun rose higher. Blue waves, green waves swept a quick fan over the beach, circling the spike of sea-holly and leaving shallow pools of light here and there on the sand.

The light touched something green in the window corner. It sharpened the edges of chairs and tables and stitched white table-cloths with fine gold wires. Everything became slightly amorphous, as if the china of the plate flowed and the steel of the knife were liquid. Meanwhile the waves breaking fell with muffled thuds, like logs falling, on the shore.

'Everybody seems to be doing things for this moment only; and never again,' said Bernard. 'Never again. The urgency of it all is fearful. Everybody knows I am going to school, going to school for the first time. 'That boy is going to school for the first time', says the housemaid, cleaning the steps. I must not cry. I must behold them indifferently.'

'Now the awful portals of the station gape; 'the moon-faced clock regards me'. I must make phrases and phrases and so interpose something hard between myself and the stare of clocks, staring faces, indifferent faces, or I shall cry. There is

Louis, there is Neville, in long coats, carrying handbags, by the booking-office. They are composed. But they look different.'

'Here is Bernard,' said Louis. 'He is composed; he is easy. He swings his bag as he walks. I will follow Bernard, because he is not afraid.'

'We are drawn through the booking-office on to the platform as a stream draws twigs and straws round the piers of a bridge,' said Neville. 'There is the very powerful, bottle-green engine without a neck, all back and thighs, breathing steam. The guard blows his whistle; the flag is dipped; without an effort, of its own momentum, like an avalanche started by a gentle push, we start forward.'

'After all this hubbub,' said Neville, all this scuffling and hubbub, we have arrived. This is indeed a moment – this is indeed a solemn moment.'

'Old Crane,' said Bernard, 'now rises to address us. Old Crane, the Headmaster, has a nose like a mountain at sunset, and a blue cleft in his chin, like a wooded ravine. He sways slightly, mouthing out his tremendous and sonorous words. I love tremendous and sonorous words. But his words are too hearty to be true. Yet he is by this time convinced of their truth. And when he leaves the room, lurching rather heavily from side to side, and hurls his way through the swing-doors, all the masters, lurching rather heavily from side to side, hurl themselves also through the swing-doors. This is our first night at school, apart from our sisters.'

'This is my first night at school,' said Susan. 'I hate the smell of pine and linoleum. I hate the wind-bitten shrubs and the sanitary tiles. I hate the cheerful jokes and the glazed look of everyone. Rhoda and Jinny sit far off in brown serge, and look at Miss Lambert who sits under a picture of Queen Alexandra reading from a book before her. If I do not purse my lips, if I do not screw my handkerchief, I shall cry.'

'The purple light,' said Rhoda, 'in Miss Lambert's ring passes to and fro across the black stain on the white page of the Prayer Book. It is a vinous, it is an amorous light. There are

desks with wells for the ink. We shall write our exercises in ink here. But here I am nobody. I have no face. This great company, all dressed in brown serge, has robbed me of my identity.'

'That dark woman,' said Jinny, 'with high cheek-bones has a shiny dress, like a shell, veined, for wearing in the evening. That is nice for summer, but for winter I should like a thin dress shot with red threads that would gleam in the firelight. Then when the lamps were lit, I should put on my red dress and it would be thin as a veil, and would wind about my body, and billow out as I came into the room, pirouetting. It would make a flower shape as I sank down, in the middle of the room, on a gilt chair. And now we pray.'

'Now we march, two by two,' said Louis, 'orderly, processional, into chapel. I like the dimness that falls as we enter the sacred building. I like the orderly progress. We file in; we seat ourselves. I like it now, when, lurching slightly, but only from his momentum, Dr Crane mounts the pulpit and reads the lesson from a Bible spread on the back of the brass eagle. I feel come over me the sense of the earth under me, and my roots going down and down till they wrap themselves round some hardness at the centre. There is no crudity here, no sudden kisses.'

'Now I will lean sideways as if to scratch my thigh. So I shall see Percival,' said Neville. 'There he sits, upright among the smaller fry. He breathes through his straight nose rather heavily. His blue and oddly inexpressive eyes are fixed with pagan indifference upon the pillar opposite. He sees nothing; he hears nothing. He is remote from us in a pagan universe.'

'But look – he flicks his hand to the back of his neck. For such gestures one falls hopelessly in love for a lifetime. Dalton, Jones, Edgar and Bateman flick their hands to the back of their necks likewise. But they do not succeed.'

'At last,' said Bernard, 'the growl ceases. The sermon ends. He has minced the dance of the white butterflies at the door to powder.'

'I note the fact for future reference with many others in my notebook. When I am grown up I shall carry a notebook – a fat book with many pages, methodically lettered. I shall enter my phrases. Under B shall come "Butterfly powder". If, in my novel, I describe the sun on the window-sill, I shall look under B and find butterfly powder. That will be useful. The tree "shades the window with green fingers". That will be useful. "The lake of my mind, unbroken by oars, heaves placidly and soon sinks into an oily somnolence." That will be useful.'

'Bernard says there is always a story,' said Neville. 'I am a story. Louis is a story.'

'There is the story of the boot-boy, the story of the man with one eye. Let him burble on with his story while I lie back and regard the stiff-legged figures of the padded batsmen through the trembling grasses. We all feel Percival lying heavy among us. But now he is chewing a stalk between his teeth. He feels bored; I too feel bored. Bernard at once perceives that we are bored. The sentence tails off feebly. Yes, the appalling moment has come when Bernard's power fails him and there is no longer any sequence and he sags and twiddles a bit of string and falls silent, gaping as if about to burst into tears. Among the tortures and devastations of life is this then – our friends are not able to finish their stories.'

'Each night I tear off the old day from the calendar, and screw it tight into a ball,' said Susan. 'I do this vindictively, while Betty and Clara are on their knees. I do not pray. I revenge myself upon the day. I wreak my spite upon its image. You are dead now, I say, school day, hated day. They have made all the days of June – this is the twenty-fifth – shiny and orderly, with gongs, with lessons, with orders to wash, to change, to work, to eat.'

'I hate the small looking-glass on the stairs,' said Jinny. 'It shows our heads only. And my lips are too wide, and my eyes are too close together; I show my gums too much when I laugh. So I skip up to the next landing, where the long glass hangs and I see myself entire.'

'At home the hay waves over the meadows,' said Susan. 'My father leans upon the stile, smoking. In the house one door bangs and then another, as the summer air puffs along the empty passages. Some old picture perhaps swings on the wall. A petal drops from the rose in the jar. All this I see, I always see, as I pass the looking-glass on the landing, with Jinny in front and Rhoda lagging behind.'

'That is my face,' said Rhoda, 'in the looking-glass behind Susan's shoulder – that face is my face. But I am not here. I have no face. Other people have faces; Susan and Jinny have faces; they are here. Their world is the real world. The things they lift are heavy. They say Yes, they say No; whereas I shift and change and am seen through in a second. Therefore I hate looking-glasses which show me my real face. Alone, I often fall down into nothingness. I must push my foot stealthily lest I should fall off the edge of the world into nothingness. I have to bang my hand against some hard door to call myself back to the body.'

❨ *I loved his voice on the stair, his old shoes and moments of being together. I think of death sometimes as the end of an excursion which I went on when he died. As if I should come in and say well, here you are.* ❨

'My soles tingle, as if wire rings opened and shut in my feet,' said Jinny. 'I see every blade of grass very clear. But the pulse drums so in my forehead, behind my eyes, that everything dances – the net, the grass; your faces leap like butterflies; the trees seem to jump up and down. There is nothing staid, nothing settled, in this universe.'

'I will make images of all the things I hate most and bury them in the ground,' said Susan. 'This shiny pebble is Madame Carlo, and I will bury her deep because of the sixpence she gave me for keeping my knuckles flat when I played my scales. I buried her sixpence. I would bury the whole school: the gymnasium; the classroom; the dining-room that always smells of meat; and the chapel. I would bury the red-brown tiles and the oily portraits of old men – benefactors, founders of schools. I would bury it all as I bury these ugly stones that are always scattered about this briny coast, with its piers and its trippers. At home, the waves are a mile long. On winter nights we hear them booming. Last Christmas a man was drowned sitting alone in his cart.'

'There are hours and hours,' said Rhoda, 'before I can put out the light and lie suspended on my bed above the world, before I can let the day drop down.'

'But as I wash, as I bend my head down over the basin, I will let the Russian Empress's veil flow about my shoulders. The diamonds of the Imperial crown blaze on my forehead. I hear the roar of the hostile mob as I step out on to the balcony. Now I dry my hands, vigorously, so that Miss, whose name I forget, cannot suspect that I am waving my fist at an infuriated mob. "I am your Empress, people." My attitude is one of defiance. I am fearless. I conquer. It is not solid; it gives me no satisfaction – this Empress dream. It leaves me, now that it has fallen, here in the passage rather shivering. Things seem paler. I will go now into the library and take out some book, and read and look; and read again and look.'

Here is a poem about a hedge. I will wander down it and pick flowers, green cowbind and the moonlight-coloured May, wild roses and ivy serpentine. I will clasp them in my hands and lay them on the desk's shiny surface.'

'This is the last day of the last term,' said Louis. 'The masters stay, we depart.'

'Here are the boxes here are the cabs,' said Neville. 'There is Percival in his billycock hat. He will forget me. He will leave my letters lying about among guns and dogs unanswered. I shall send him poems and he will perhaps reply with a picture postcard. But it is for that that I love him. I shall propose meeting – under a clock, by some Cross; and shall wait, and he will not come. It is for that that I love him. Oblivious, almost entirely ignorant, he will pass from my life. And I shall pass, incredible as it seems, into other lives. I feel already that things we have only dimly perceived draw near.'

36

'Now we are off,' said Louis. 'Now I hang suspended without attachments. We are passing through England in a train. And I have no firm ground to which I go. Bernard and Neville, Percival, Archie, Larpent and Baker go to Oxford or Cambridge. I go vaguely, to make money vaguely. I force myself to mark this inch in the long, long history that began in Egypt, in the time of the Pharoahs. But the chained beast stamps on the beach. It stamps and stamps.'

'Now I will let myself lean out of the window,' said Susan. 'The air rushes down my nose and throat – the cold air, the salt air with the smell of turnip fields in it. And there is my father, with his back turned, talking to a farmer. I tremble, I cry. There is my father in gaiters. There is my father.'

'Now we roar and swing into a tunnel,' said Jinny. 'There is then a great society of bodies, and mine is introduced; mine has come into the room where the gilt chairs are.'

'Also, in the middle, cadaverous, awful, lay the grey puddle in the courtyard, when, holding an envelope in my hand, I carried a message. I could not cross it. Identity failed me. We are nothing.'

'This is life then to which I am committed.'

'It is the first day of the summer holidays,' said Rhoda, 'And now, as the train passes by these red rocks, by this blue sea, the term, done with, forms itself into one shape behind me.'

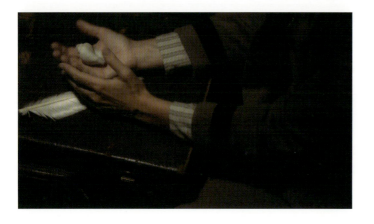

'Now we draw near the centre of the civilized world,' said Neville. 'There are the familiar gasometers. There are the public gardens intersected by asphalt paths. There are the lovers lying shamelessly mouth to mouth on the burnt grass. The train slows and lengthens, as we approach London, the centre. What extraordinary adventure waits me, among these mail vans, these porters, these swarms of people calling taxis? The huge uproar is in my ears. It sounds and resounds under this glass roof like the surge of a sea. We are cast down on the platform with our handbags. My sense of self almost perishes. I become drawn in, tossed down, thrown sky-high. I step out on to the platform, grasping tightly all that I possess – one bag.'

THREE

The sun rose. Light almost pierced the thin swift waves as they raced fan-shaped over the beach.

Now, too, the rising sun came in at the window, touching the red-edged curtain and the looking-glass whitened its pool upon the wall. A plate was like a white lake. Tables and chairs rose to the surface as if they had been sunk under water.

'The complexity of things becomes more close,' said Bernard, 'here at college, where the stir and pressure of life are so extreme, where the excitement of mere living becomes daily more urgent. Especially now, when I have left a room, and people talking, and the stone flags ring out with my solitary footsteps, and I behold the moon rising, sublimely, indifferently, over the ancient chapel – then it becomes clear that I am not one and simple, but complex and many.'

'I am now in the mood, I can write the letter straight off which I have begun ever so many times. I have just come in; I have flung down my hat and my stick; I am writing the first thing that comes into my head without troubling to put the paper straight. It is going to be a brilliant sketch which, she must think, was written without a pause, without an erasure. Look how unformed the letters are – there is a careless blot. All must be sacrificed to speed and carelessness. I will write a quick, running, small hand, exaggerating the down stroke of the "y" and crossing the "t" thus – with a dash. The date shall be only Tuesday, the 17th, and then a question mark. But also I must give her the impression that though he – for this is not myself – is writing in such an off-hand, such a slap-dash way, there is some subtle suggestion of intimacy and respect. I must allude to talks we have had together – bring back some remembered scene. But I must seem to her (this is very important) to be passing from thing to thing with the greatest ease in the world. I shall pass from the service for the man who was drowned (I have a phrase for that) to Mrs Moffat and her sayings (I have a note of them), and so to some reflections apparently casual but full of profundity (profound criticism is often written casually) about some book I have been

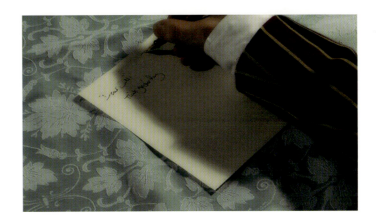

reading, some out-of-the-way book. I want her to say as she brushes her hair or puts out the candle, "Where did I read that? Oh, in Bernard's letter." It is the speed, the hot, molten effect, the laval flow of sentence into sentence that I need. Who am I thinking of? Byron of course. I am, in some ways, like Byron. Perhaps a sip of Byron will help to put me in the vein. Let me read a page. No; this is dull; this is scrappy. This is rather too formal. Now I am getting the hang of it. Now I am getting his beat into my brain (the rhythm is the main thing in writing). Now, without pausing I will begin, on the very lilt of the stroke –'

'Look how a boat passes, filled with indolent, with unconscious, with powerful young men,' said Neville. 'They are listening to the gramophone; they are eating fruit out of paper bags. They are tossing the skins of bananas, which then sink eel-like, into the river. All they do is beautiful. That is Percival, lounging on the cushions, monolithic, in giant repose. No, it is only one of his satellites, imitating his monolithic, his giant repose.'

'Let us go back together, over the bridge, under the elm trees, to my room,' said Bernard, 'where, with walls round us and red serge curtains drawn, we can shut out these distracting voices, scents and savours of lime trees, and other lives; these furtive glimpses of some vague and vanishing figure – it might be Jinny, it might be Susan, or was that Rhoda disappearing down the avenue?'

'I hate your greasy handkerchiefs – you will stain your copy of Don Juan,' said Neville. 'You are not listening to me. You are making phrases about Byron. And while you gesticulate, with your cloak, your cane, I am trying to expose a secret told to nobody yet; I am asking you to take my life in your hands and tell me whether I am doomed always to cause repulsion in those I love?'

'You are not listening,' said Bernard. 'You are making some protest, with an inexpressibly familiar gesture. By such signs we diagnose our friends' diseases. "Stop," you seem to say. "Ask me what I suffer."'

'Take it. Catch it – my poem.'

'You are not Byron; you are your self.'

'He has left me his poem', said Bernard. 'O friendship, I too will press flowers between the pages of Shakespeare's sonnets! I think of Louis now. What malevolent yet searching light would Louis throw upon this dwindling autumn evening, upon Neville, Byron and our life here?'

'People go on passing,' said Louis. 'They pass the window of this eating-shop incessantly. In the background I perceive shops and houses; also the grey spires of a city church. In the foreground are glass shelves set with plates of buns and ham sandwiches. All is somewhat obscured by steam from a tea-urn.'

'I prop my book against a bottle of Worcester sauce and try to look like the rest. Yet I cannot. They are discussing the sale of a piano. It blocks up the hall. People go on passing; they go on passing against the spires of the church and the plates of ham sandwiches. I cannot therefore concentrate on my dinner. "The case is handsome; but it blocks up the hall." Meanwhile the hats bob up and down; the door perpetually shuts and opens. I am conscious of flux, of disorder; of annihilation and despair. If this is all, this is worthless. "Bring us back to the fold, we who pass so disjectedly, bobbing up and down, past windows with plates of ham sandwiches in the foreground." Yes; I will reduce you to order.'

'My roots go down through veins of lead and silver to a knot made of oak roots bound together in the centre. Sealed and blind, with earth stopping my ears; I have seen women carrying red pitchers to the banks of the Nile. I woke in a garden, with a blow on the nape of my neck, a hot kiss, Jinny's. I see the gleaming tea-urn; the glass cases full of pale-yellow sandwiches; the men in round coats perched on stools at the counter; and also behind them, eternity.'

'I think sometimes (I am not twenty yet) I am not a woman, but the light that falls on this gate, on this ground,' said Susan. 'I am the seasons, I think sometimes, January, May, November; the mud, the mist, the dawn. I cannot be tossed about, or float gently, or mix with other people. Yet now, leaning here till the gate prints my arm, I feel the weight that has formed itself in my side. I shall be like my mother, silent in a blue apron locking up the cupboards.'

'At Elvedon the gardeners swept and swept with their great brooms, and the woman sat at a table writing.'

'I sit waiting for my father's footsteps as he shuffles down the passage pinching some herb between his fingers. I pour out cup after cup while the unopened flowers hold themselves erect on the table among the pots of jam, the loaves and the butter.'

'We are silent.'

◖ *My first memory of her is of her lap; the scratch of some beads on her dress comes back to me as I pressed my cheek against it. Then I see her in her white dressing gown; and the passion flower with a purple star on its petals. I no longer hear her voice; I do not see her.* ◖

'Evening comes and the lamps are lit. And when evening comes and the lamps are lit they make a yellow fire in the ivy. I sit with my sewing by the table. I think of Jinny; of Rhoda; and hear the rattle of wheels on the pavement as the farm horses plod home. I hear traffic roaring in the evening wind. I look at the quivering leaves in the dark garden and think "They dance in London. Jinny kisses Louis."'

'I feel myself shining in the dark,' said Jinny. 'Silk is on my knee. My silk legs rub smoothly together. The stones of a necklace lie cold on my throat. My feet feel the pinch of shoes. I sit bolt upright so that my hair may not touch the back of the seat. I am arrayed, I am prepared. This is the momentary pause; the dark moment. The fiddlers have lifted their bows.'

'Now the car slides to a stop. A strip of pavement is lighted. I enter.'

'Here are gilt chairs in the empty, the expectant rooms, and flowers, stiller, statelier, than flowers that grow, spread against the walls. I am a native of this world. Here is my risk, here is my adventure. The door opens. O come, I say to this one, rippling gold from head to heels. "Come," and he comes towards me.'

'I shall edge behind them,' said Rhoda, 'as if I saw someone I know. But I know no one. I shall twitch the curtain and look at the moon. Let me visit furtively the treasures I have laid apart. Pools lie on the other side of the world reflecting marble columns. The swallow dips her wing in dark pools.'

'I am thrust back to stand burning in this clumsy, this ill-fitting body, to receive the shafts of his indifference and his scorn, I who long for marble columns and pools on the other side of the world where the swallow dips her wings.'

'Alone, I rock my basins; I am mistress of my fleet of ships. What is the knowledge that Jinny has as she dances; the assurance that Susan has as, stooping quietly beneath the lamplight, she draws the white cotton through the eye of her needle? They say, Yes; they say, No; they bring their fists down with a bang on the table. But I doubt; I tremble; I see the wild thorn tree shake its shadow in the desert.'

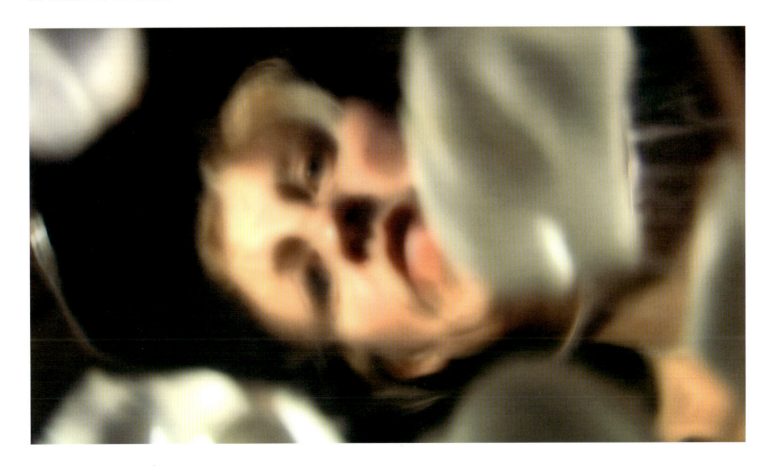

FOUR

The sun had risen to its full height – uncompromising, undeniable. It struck upon the hard sand, and showed the white bone, or the boot without laces stuck, black as iron, in the sand. The waves broke and spread their waters swiftly over the shore.

The sun struck straight upon the house, making the white walls glare between the dark windows. Sharp-edged wedges of light lay upon the window-sill. Behind hung a zone of shadow – dense depths of darkness.

'How fair, how strange,' said Bernard, 'glittering, many-pointed and many-domed London lies before me under mist. Guarded by gasometers, by factory chimneys, she lies sleeping as we approach. The early train from the north is hurled at her like a missile. We draw a curtain as we pass. Blank expectant faces stare at us as we rattle and flash through stations. Men clutch their newspapers a little tighter, as our wind sweeps them, envisaging death. But we roar on. We are about to explode in the flanks of the city like a shell in the side of some ponderous, maternal, majestic animal.'

'I think of people to whom I could say things: Louis, Neville, Susan, Jinny and Rhoda. With them I am many-sided. They retrieve me from darkness. We shall meet tonight, thank Heaven. Thank Heaven, I need not be alone. We shall dine together. We shall say good-bye to Percival, who goes to India.'

'It is now five minutes to eight,' said Neville. 'I have come early. I have taken my place at the table ten minutes before the time in order to taste every moment of anticipation; to see the door open and to say, "Is it Percival? No; it is not Percival." I have seen the door open and shut twenty times already; each time the suspense sharpens. This is the place to which he is coming. This is the table at which he will sit. Here, incredible as it seems, will be his actual body. This table, these chairs, this metal vase with its three red flowers are about to undergo an extraordinary transformation.'

The door opens, but he does not come. That is Louis hesitating there. He looks at himself in the looking-glass as he comes in; he touches his hair; he is dissatisfied with his appearance. He has seen me. Here he is.'

'There is Susan,' said Louis. 'She does not see us. She has not dressed, because she despises the futility of London. She stands for a moment at the swing-door, looking about her like a creature dazed by the light of a lamp. Now she moves. She seems to find her way by instinct in and out among these little tables, touching no one, disregarding waiters, yet comes straight to our table in the corner. When she sees us (Neville, and myself) her face assumes a certainty which is alarming, as if she had what she wanted. To be loved by Susan would be to be impaled by a bird's sharp beak, to be nailed to a barnyard door. Yet there are moments when I could wish to be speared by a beak, to be nailed to a barnyard door, positively, once and for all.'

'Rhoda comes now, from nowhere, having slipped in while we were not looking,' said Susan. 'She must have made a torturous course, so as to put off as long as possible the shock of recognition, so as to be secure for one more moment to rock her petals in her basin.'

'The door opens, the door goes on opening,' said Neville. 'Yet he does not come.'

'There is Jinny,' said Rhoda. 'She seems to centre every-thing; round her tables, lines of doors, windows, ceilings, ray themselves, like rays round the star in the middle of a smashed window-pane. Now she sees us and moves. We change.'

'He has not come,' said Neville. 'The door opens and he does not come. That is Bernard. He hesitates on his way here. Who is that? he asks himself, for he half knows a woman in an opera cloak. He half knows everybody; he knows nobody. But now, perceiving us, he waves a benevolent salute; he bears down.'

'Now we are together. But without Percival there is no solidity. We are silhouettes, hollow phantoms moving mistily without a background.'

'The sharp breath of his misery scatters my being,' said Rhoda. 'Nothing can settle; nothing can subside. Every time the door opens he looks fixedly at the table – he dare not raise his eyes – then looks for one second and says, "He has not come". But here he is.'

'Now,' said Neville, 'the reign of chaos is over. He has imposed order. Knives cut again.'

'Here and now we are together,' said Bernard. 'We have come together, at a particular time, to this particular spot. We are drawn into this communion by some deep, some common emotion. Shall we call it, conveniently, "love"? Shall we say "love of Percival" because Percival is going to India? There is a red carnation in that vase. A single flower as we sat here waiting, but now a seven-sided flower, many-petalled, red – a whole flower to which every eye brings its own contribution. At Elvedon the gardeners swept and swept with their great brooms. And the woman sat writing.'

'I like to be with people who twist herbs, and spit into the fire, and shuffle down long passages in slippers like my father,' said Susan. 'The only sayings I understand are cries of love, hate, rage and pain. This talking is undressing an old woman whose dress seems to be part of her, but now, as we talk, she turns pinkish underneath, and has wrinkled thighs and sagging breasts.'

'We differ, it may be too profoundly,' said Louis, 'for explanation. But let us attempt it. I smoothed my hair when I came in, hoping to look like the rest of you. But I cannot, for I am not single and entire as you are. I find relics of myself in the sand that women made thousands of years ago, when I heard songs by the Nile and the chained beast stamping. But while I admire Susan and Percival, I hate the others, because it is for them that I do these antics, smoothing my hair, concealing my accent.'

'But when you stand in the door,' said Neville, 'you inflict stillness, demanding admiration, and that is a great impediment. I shall never have what I want. The swiftness of my mind is too strong for my body. I excite pity in the crises of life, not love.'

'But you will never hate me,' said Jinny. 'I can imagine nothing beyond the circle cast by my body. My body goes before me, like a lantern down a dark lane, bringing one thing after another out of darkness into a ring of light. I dazzle you. The leaf danced in the hedge without anyone to blow it.'

'And I picked all the petals and made them swim,' said Rhoda. 'Nothing persists. One moment does not lead to another. The door opens and the tiger leaps. You did not see me come. I circled round the chairs to avoid the horror of the spring. I am afraid of you all. I am afraid of the shock of sensation that leaps upon me, because I cannot deal with it as you do – I cannot make one moment merge in the next. To me they are all violent, all separate; and if I fall under the shock of the leap of the moment you will be on me, tearing me to pieces. I have no end in view. I do not know how to run minute to minute and hour to hour, solving them by some natural force until they make the whole and indivisible mass that you call life. Because you have an end in view – one person, is it, to sit beside, an idea is it, your beauty is it? And I have no face. I am like the foam that races over the beach. I am whirled down caverns, and flap like paper against endless corridors, and must press my hand against the wall to draw myself back.'

'See how she grasps her fork,' said Bernard, 'her weapon against us.'

'It is Percival,' said Louis, 'sitting silent as he sat among the tickling grasses when the breeze parted the clouds and they formed again, who makes us aware that these attempts to say, "I am this, I am that", which we make, coming together, like separated parts of one body and soul, are false. Something has been left out from fear. We have tried to accentuate differences from the desire to be separate. But there is a chain whirling round, round, in a steel-blue circle beneath.'

'It is hate, it is love,' said Susan. 'That is the furious coal-black stream that makes us dizzy if we look down into it. We stand on a ledge here, but if we look down we turn giddy. Through the chink in the hedge I saw her kiss him'.

'It is love,' said Jinny, 'it is hate, such as Susan feels for me because I kissed Louis once in the garden; because equipped as I am, I make her think when I come in, "My hands are red," and hide them. But our hatred is almost indistinguishable from our love.'

'Yet these roaring waters,' said Neville, 'upon which we build our crazy platforms are more stable than the wild, the weak and inconsequent cries that we utter when, trying to speak, we rise; when we reason and jerk out these false sayings, "I am this; I am that!" Speech is false. I look steadily into the mill-race that foams beneath. By what particular name are we to call it? Let Rhoda speak. Love is not a whirlpool to her. She is not giddy when she looks down. She looks far away over our heads, beyond India.'

'Yes, between your shoulders, over your heads, to a landscape,' said Rhoda, 'to a hollow where the many-backed steep hills come down like birds' wings folded. There, on the short, firm turf, are bushes, dark leaved, and against their darkness I see a shape, white, but not of stone, moving, perhaps alive. But it is not you, it is not you, it is not you; not Percival, Susan, Jinny, Neville or Louis. It makes no sign, it does not beckon, it does not see us. Behind it roars the sea. It is beyond our reach.'

'Look, Rhoda,' said Louis, 'their eyes are like moth's wings moving so quickly that they do not seem to move at all.'

'Death is woven in with the violets,' said Rhoda. 'Death and again death.'

'And sometimes I begin to doubt if there are stories. What is my story? What is Rhoda's? What is Neville's? There are facts, as, for example: "The handsome young man in the grey suit, whose reserve contrasted so strangely with the loquacity of the others, now brushed the crumbs from his waistcoat and, with a characteristic gesture, at once commanding and benign, made a sign to the waiter, who came instantly and returned a moment later with the bill discreetly folded upon a plate." That is the truth; that is a fact, but beyond it all is darkness and conjecture.'

'Now once more,' said Louis, 'as we are about to part, having paid our bill, the circle in our blood, broken so often, so sharply, for we are so different, closes in a ring. Something is made. Yes, as we rise and fidget, a little nervously, we pray, holding in our hands this common feeling. Do not move, do not let the swing door cut to pieces the thing that we have made, that globes itself here, among these lights, these peelings, this litter of bread crumbs and people passing. Do not move, do not go. Hold it for ever.'

'Let us hold it for one moment,' said Jinny.

'Forests and far countries on the other side of the world,' said Rhoda, 'are in it; seas and jungles; the howlings of jackals and moonlight falling upon some high peak where the eagle soars.'

'Happiness is in it,' said Neville, 'and the quiet of ordinary things. A table, a chair, a book with a paper-knife stuck between the pages. And the petal falling from the rose, and the light flickering as we sit silent, or, perhaps, bethinking us of some trifle, suddenly speak.'

'Week-days are in it,' said Susan, 'Monday, Tuesday, Wednesday; the horses going up to the fields, and the horses returning; the rooks rising and falling, and catching the elm-trees in their net, whether it is April, whether it is November.'

'What is to come is in it,' said Bernard. 'That is the last drop and the brightest that we let fall like some supernal quicksilver into the swelling and splendid moment created by us from Percival. What is to come? I ask, what is outside?'

'Now the agony begins; now the horror has seized me,' said Neville. 'Now the cab comes; now Percival goes. What can we do to keep him? How signal to all time to come that we, who stand in the street, in the lamplight, loved Percival? Now Percival is gone.'

FIVE

The sun no longer stood in the middle of the sky. Its light slanted, falling obliquely. The waves massed themselves, curved their backs and crashed. They fell like the thud of a great beast stamping.

The blind hung red at the window's edge and within the room daggers of light fell upon chairs and tables making cracks across their lacquer and polish.

'He is dead.' said Neville. 'He fell. His horse tripped. He was thrown. The sails of the world have swung round and caught me on the head. All is over. The lights of the world have gone out. There stands the tree which I cannot pass. I will not lift my foot to climb the stair. I will stand for one moment beneath the immitigable tree, alone with the man whose throat is cut, while downstairs the cook shoves in and out the dampers. I will not climb the stair. We are doomed, all of us. Women shuffle past with shopping-bags. People keep on passing.'

❦ Every day includes much more non-being than being. Yesterday, for example . . . although it was a good day, the goodness was embedded in a kind of nondescript cotton wool. This is always so. A great part of every day is not lived consciously. One walks, eats, sees things, deals with what has to be done; the broken vacuum cleaner; ordering dinner; writing orders to Mabel. ❦

'Where shall I go now then?' said Rhoda. 'To some museum, where they keep rings under glass cases, where there are cabinets, and the dresses that queens have worn? Or shall I go to Hampton Court? There shall I recover beauty, and impose order upon my raked, my dishevelled soul? But what can one make in loneliness? Alone I should stand on the empty grass and say, Rooks fly; somebody passes with a bag; there is a gardener with a wheelbarrow.'

'I should stand in a queue and smell sweat, and scent as horrible as sweat; and be hung with other people like a joint of meat among other joints of meat.'

'There is the puddle, and I cannot cross it. I hear the rush of the great grindstone within an inch of my head. Its wind roars in my face. All palpable forms of life have failed me. Unless I can stretch and touch something hard, I shall be blown down the eternal corridors for ever. What, then, can I touch? What brick, what stone? and so draw myself across the enormous gulf into my body safely?'

'I pad about the house all day long in apron and slippers, like my mother who died of cancer,' said Susan.' Whether it is summer, whether it is winter, I no longer know by the moor grass, and the heath flower; only by the steam on the window-pane, or the frost on the window-pane.'

'Look at the street now that Percival is dead,' said Rhoda. 'Percival, by his death, has made me this present, has revealed this terror – faces and faces, coarse, greedy, casual; looking in at shop-windows with pendant parcels; ogling, brushing, destroying everything, leaving even our love impure, touched now by their dirty fingers. Here is the shop where they sell stockings. The moon rises through blue seas alone and pools lie on the other side of the world reflecting marble columns. The swallow dips her wings in distant pools. And I could believe that beauty is once more set flowing. Its whisper comes down these aisles, through these laces, breathing among baskets of coloured ribbons.'

'Pain is suspended as a girl silently slides open a drawer. And then, she speaks; her voice wakes me. I shoot to the bottom among the weeds and see envy, jealousy, hatred and spite scuttle like crabs over the sand as she speaks. These are our companion's. I will pay my bill and take my parcel.'

'I love punctually at ten to come into my room', said Louis, 'I love the purple glow of the dark mahogany; I love the table and its sharp edge; and the smooth-running drawers. I love the telephone with its lip stretched to my whisper, and the date on the wall; and the engagement book. Mr Prentice at four; Mr Eyres sharp at four-thirty. I have helped to score those lines on the map there by which the different parts of the world are laced together.'

'Into the wave that dashes upon the shore,' said Rhoda, 'into the wave that flings its white foam to the uttermost corners of the earth, I throw my violets, my offering to Percival.'

SIX

The sun had now sunk lower in the sky. The clouds drew themselves across the sun so that the rocks went suddenly black and shadows were blown like grey cloths over the sea.

The red curtains and the white blinds blew in and out, flapping against the edge of the window. All for a moment wavered and bent in uncertainty, as if a great moth sailing through the room had shadowed the immense solidity of chairs and tables with floating wings.

'And time,' said Bernard, 'lets fall its drop. The drop that has formed on the roof of the soul falls. On the roof of my mind time, forming, lets fall its drop.'

'Last week, as I stood shaving, the drop fell. I, standing with my razor in my hand, became suddenly aware of the merely habitual nature of my action (this is the drop forming) and congratulated my hands, ironically, for keeping at it. Shave, shave, shave, I said. Go on shaving. The drop fell. And as I buttoned on my coat to go home I said more dramatically, "I have lost my youth."'

'It is curious how, at every crisis, some phrase which does not fit insists upon coming to the rescue – the penalty of living in an old civilization with a notebook. This drop falling has nothing to do with losing my youth. This drop falling is time tapering to a point.'

'Now I sit here like a convalescent, like a very simple man who knows only words of one syllable. "The sun is hot," I say. "The wind is cold." I feel myself carried round like an insect on top of the earth and could swear that, sitting here, I feel its hardness, its turning movement. I see far out a waste of water. A fin turns. This bare visual impression is unattached to any line of reason, it springs up as one might see the fin of a porpoise on the horizon. I note under F., therefore, "fin in a waste of waters." I, who am perpetually making notes in the margin of my mind for some final statement, make this mark, waiting for some winter's evening.'

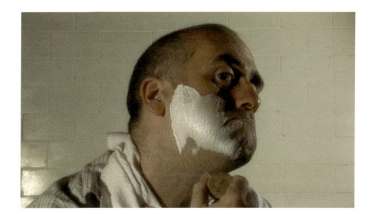

'I ask now,' said Susan, standing with my scissors among my flowers. 'Where can the shadow enter? What shock can loosen my laboriously gathered, relentlessly pressed down life? Yet sometimes I am sick of natural happiness, and fruit growing, and children scattering the house with oars, guns, skulls, books won for prizes and other trophies.'

'I am fenced in, planted here like one of my own trees. I think sometimes of Percival who loved me. He rode and fell in India. I think sometimes of Rhoda. Uneasy cries wake me at dead of night.'

'The fixity of my morning broke and, putting down the bag of flour, I remembered the wandering lights upon the skeleton roots of the beech trees where I sat, sobbing. And how we went to Elvedon and trod on rotten oak-apples, and saw the lady writing and the gardeners with their great brooms. And I thought, Life stands round me now like glass round the imprisoned reed.'

'Here I stand,' said Jinny, 'in the tube, where everything that is desirable meets. I stand for a moment under the pavement in the heart of London. Innumerable wheels rush and feet press just over my head. The great avenues of civilization meet here and strike this way and that. I am in the heart of life.'

'But look – there is my body in that looking glass. How solitary, how shrunk, how aged! I am no longer young. I am no longer part of the procession. Millions descend those stairs in a terrible descent. Great wheels churn inexorably urging them downwards. Millions have died. Percival died. I still move. I still live. But who will come if I signal?'

'There will be no reflections in window-panes in dark tunnels. I will fill the vases with lavish, with luxurious, with extravagant flowers nodding in great bunches. I will put ready cigarettes, glasses and some gaily covered new unread book in case Bernard comes, or Neville or Louis. But perhaps it will not be Bernard, Neville or Louis, but somebody new, somebody unknown, somebody I passed on a staircase and, just turning as we passed, I murmured, "Come." Let the silent army of the dead descend. I march forward.'

'I pass Jinny's house without envy,' said Neville. 'And smile at the young man who arranges his tie a little nervously on the door-step.'

'There are people talking, or hardly troubling to talk. He says, she says, somebody else says things have been said so often that one word is now enough to lift a whole weight. I take a book and read half a page of anything. They have not mended the spout of the teapot yet. The child dances, dressed in her mother's clothes.'

'But then Rhoda, or it may be Louis, some fasting and anguished spirit, passes through and out again. They want a plot, do they? They want a reason? It is not enough for them, this ordinary scene.'

'Yet if they want violence, I have seen death and murder and suicide all
in one room. One comes in, one goes out. There are sobs on the staircase.
I have heard threads broken and knots tied and the quiet stitching of white
cambric going on and on, on the knees of a woman.'

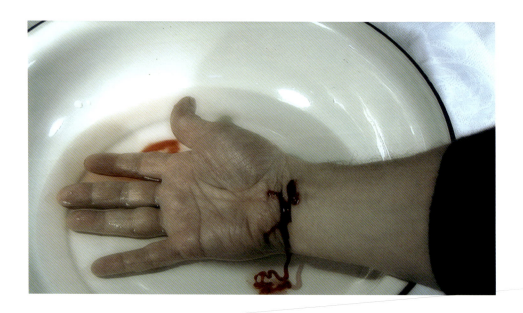

'Why ask, like Louis, for a reason, or fly like Rhoda to some far grove and part the leaves of the laurels and look for statues? Rhoda flies with her neck outstretched and blind fanatic eyes. Louis, now so opulent, goes to his attic window among the blistered roofs and gazes where she has vanished, but must sit down in his office among the typewriters and the telephone and work it all out for our instruction, for our regeneration, and the reform of an unborn world.'

'I open a little book,' said Louis. 'I read one poem. One poem is enough.

  O western wind, when wilt thou blow . . .
  That the small rain down can rain?'

'Life has been a terrible affair for me. I am like some vast sucker, some glutinous, some adhesive, some insatiable mouth. I have tried to draw from the living flesh the stone lodged at the centre.'

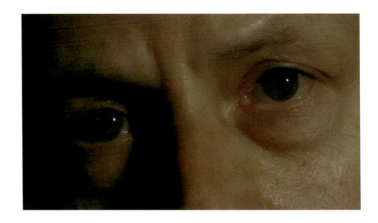

'Rhoda left me. Rhoda, with whom I shared silence when the others spoke, she has gone now like the desert heat. When the sun blisters the roofs of the city I think of her; when the dry leaves patter to the ground; when the old men come with pointed sticks and pierce little bits of paper as we pierced her –

  O western wind, when wilt thou blow,
    That the small rain down can rain?
    Christ, that my love were in my arms,
    And I in my bed again!'

'I return now to my book; I return now to my attempt.'

'There is only a thin sheet between me now and the infinite depths,' said Rhoda.
'The lumps in the mattress soften beneath me.'

'My path has been up and up, towards some solitary tree with a pool beside it on the very top. When the wind stoops to brush this height, may there be nothing found but a pinch of dust.'

'I launch out now over the precipice. Beneath me lies the lights of the herring fleet. The cliffs vanish. Rippling small, rippling grey, innumerable waves spread beneath me. I touch nothing. I see nothing. I may sink and settle on the waves. The sea will drum in my ears. The white petals will be darkened with sea water. They will float for a moment and then sink. Rolling me over the waves will shoulder me under. Everything falls in a tremendous shower, dissolving me.'

SEVEN

The waves, as they neared the shore, fell in one long concussion, like a wall falling, a wall of grey stone, unpierced by any chink of light. The blackness on the beach deepened.

A breeze rose; a shiver ran through the leaves.

'The tone of my voice as I say "Hampton Court" proves that I am middle-aged,' said Bernard. 'Ten years, fifteen years ago, I should have said "Hampton Court?" with interrogation – what will it be like? Will there be lakes, mazes? Or with anticipation, What is going to happen to me here? Whom shall I meet? Now, Hampton Court – Hampton Court – the words beat a gong in the space which I have so laboriously cleared with half a dozen telephone messages and postcards: and pictures rise – summer afternoons, boats, old ladies holding their skirts up, one urn in winter, some daffodils in March – these all float to the top of the waters that now lie deep on every scene.'

'There at the door by the Inn, our meeting-place, they are already standing – Susan, Louis, Rhoda and Neville. They have come together already. I come nearer. They do not see me. Now Rhoda sees me, but she pretends, with her horror of the shock of meeting, that I am a stranger. Now Neville turns. Suddenly, raising my hand, saluting Neville I cry, "I too have pressed flowers between the pages of Shakespeare's sonnets," and am churned up. My little boat bobs unsteadily upon the chopped and tossing waves. There is no panacea (let me note) against the shock of meeting.'

'There were lamp-posts,' said Rhoda, 'and trees that had not yet shed their leaves on the way from the station. The leaves might have hidden me still. But I did not hide behind them. I walked straight up to you instead of circling round to avoid the shock of sensation as I used. But it is only that I have taught my body to do a certain trick. Inwardly I am not taught; I fear, I hate, I love, I envy and despise you, but I never join you happily.'

'There is always somebody, when we come together, and the edges of meeting are still sharp, who refuses to be submerged,' said Neville, 'whose identity therefore one wishes to make crouch beneath one's own. For me now, it is Susan. I talk to impress Susan. Listen to me, Susan. Let solidity be destroyed.'

'Yet look, Neville, whom I discredit in order to be myself, at my hand,' said Susan. 'Look at the gradations of healthy colour here on the knuckles, here on the palm. My body has been used daily, rightly, like a tool by a good workman, all over. The blade is clean, sharp, worn in the centre. Seen through your pale and yielding flesh, even apples and bunches of fruit must have a filmed look as if they stood under glass.'

'It is true, and I know for a fact,' said Bernard, 'as we walk down this avenue, that a King, riding, fell over a molehill here. But how strange it seems to set against the whirling abysses of infinite space a little figure with a golden teapot on his head.'

'Three hundred years now', said Neville, 'seem no more than a moment vanished against that dog. Making love to a nursemaid behind a tree, that soldier is more admirable than all the stars.'

'While we advance down this avenue,' said Louis, 'I leaning slightly upon Jinny, Bernard arm-in-arm with Neville, and Susan with her hand in mine, it is difficult not to weep, calling ourselves little children, praying that God may keep us safe while we sleep. It is sweet to sing together, clasping hands, afraid of the dark.'

'Time's fangs have ceased their devouring', said Jinny. 'We have triumphed over the abysses of space, with rouge, with powder, with flimsy pocket-handkerchiefs.'

'I grasp, I hold fast,' said Susan. 'I hold firmly to this hand,
anyone's, with love, with hatred; it does not matter which.'

'It is not often that one has no anxiety' said Rhoda, 'when the
walls of the mind become transparent.'

'At Elvedon,' said Susan, 'the gardeners swept and swept
with their great brooms and the woman sat at a great
table writing.'

¶ *To tell you the truth, I have practically no emotion left.
I . . . have not even troubled to clean my nails. I have not done
my hair. I can't believe in being anyone. When I read a book
I cannot finish it . . . Vanity of vanities, all is vanity.* ¶

'Drop upon drop,' said Bernard, 'silence falls. It forms on the roof of the mind and falls into pools beneath. For ever alone, alone, alone, – hear silence fall and sweep its rings to the farthest edges. Gorged and replete, solid with middle-aged content, I, whom loneliness destroys, let silence fall, drop by drop. I reflect now that the earth is only a pebble flicked off accidentally from the face of the sun and that there is no life anywhere in the abysses of space.'

'In this silence,' said Susan, 'it seems as if no leaf would ever
fall, or bird fly.'

'As if the miracle had happened,' said Jinny, 'and life were
stayed here and now.'

'And,' said Rhoda, 'we had no more to
live.'

'But listen,' said Louis, 'to the world moving through abysses of infinite space. It roars; the lighted strip of history is past; we are gone; our civilization; the Nile; and all life. Our separate drops are dissolved; we are extinct, lost in the abysses of time, in the darkness.'

'The door will not open; he will not come,' said Neville. 'And we are laden. Being now all of us middle-aged, loads are on us. Let us put down our loads.'

94